Discover you...

Look Inside
&
Find the Gift

Sharon Duvall

Sunny Horizon

Published by Sunny Horizon
36 Nelson Road
Newport
Isle of Wight
PO30 1RE

ISBN 978 0 9557680 0 2

Copyright Sharon Duvall 2007

The right of Sharon Duvall to be indentified as the author of this work has been asserted by her in accordance with the Copyright, Designs and Patents Act 1988.

All rights reserved. No parts of this publication may be reproduced, stored in a retrieval system or transmitted in any form or by any means, electronic, mechanical, photocopying, recording or otherwise, without the prior permission of Sharon Duvall.

Typeset and Layout by Peter Atkinson, Chale Green, Isle of Wight
Printed in Great Britain by RPM Reprographics Ltd, Chichester

Preface

This book is to guide the reader to become aware of the true presents, the magic gift within. Discover the essence inside you, your gift(s)!

For a long time, before I had even thought of this book! I had been wondering "what am I doing where am I going with my life?"

Then all of a sudden different ideas and inspiration started to come into my mind, the messages continued every night with the information and knowledge for this book and it has been a great experience bringing it all together. I have studied and researched people, language and the meaning of words and their use, bringing about amazing results. This inspired me to create some sayings of my own which are: 'Miracle swamp, Mind of magic and Miracle mind' these are terms I use in this book to explain how clever the mind really is! Also I use the word 'Amazing' a lot as that is what and how it feels! I have gone through many experiences and stages of life, from being in the miracle swamp to dancing around the edge of it, and of course, enjoying the gifts that the miracle mind does really bring!

I have put these principles into action with many people, who were very impressed and inspired with how they felt and the changes that occurred for them.

I was fortunate to acquire this knowledge and now I would like to share it with you.

I trust you will be as inspired and delighted as I was when writing it.

Acknowledgements

Many thanks to all my family and friends for their inspiration and support, it is much appreciated and has helped a great deal in producing this book.

I would especially like to thank my brother, Dave Betts, as without his financial support this book would not have been possible.

LOOK INSIDE AND FIND THE GIFT

Introduction

Whilst creating this book I spent quality time with various people guiding them to experience their lives in the way they desired them to be. Just feeling good about themselves and who they are, brought amazing results. Therefore, by following the same principles within this book you too can produce amazing effects for yourself and others around you.

Everybody who reads this book will themselves have different aspects in life that they desire or wish to improve, your own-self, relationships, careers, finances or any other prospects you have in mind. This book will show you how to experience life in a new and amazing way.

If you have picked up this book and are reading these words then there is something in this book that is a message for you!

As you read through this book, there will be times when you read certain pieces of information; it might be a good idea to think about them for a moment before reading on. The importance of this is to give yourself a bit of time to consider/contemplate what you have just been reading.

This way of being will become second nature like everything else you do in your life.

SO ENJOY!

There are three parts that make up this book, these are:

Part 1. The twists and tales of life's mysteries

The purpose of this book is to share with others the knowledge that has been shown to me over time, bringing me to where I am now in life. This book will give you guidance and show you how to let go of negativity, allowing you to discover the true you, bringing the understanding to believe in yourself and the magic gift within you.

It will also reveal how to be positive and stay that way, creating what you truly desire and deserve. Showing you how to teach yourself to balance your heart and mind to strengthen your will power and belief system, generating a new understanding with a whole new meaning allowing good things to happen to you.

Also it shows and explains the importance of language and how it is used.

Part 2. The 10 Golden Messages.

The 10 Golden Messages are short messages with big input uncovering amazing potential within you, guiding you to a better understanding of yourself. By using these guidelines you will see and feel a difference, allowing a positive outlook to generate, and discover your true self!

I have also included 10 Golden formulas, (quick reminders) of the information in the book to use as a guideline

Part 3. The Glossary.   A – Z of amazing words

The glossary started off with a dozen words, now there are over three hundred. I discovered a lot about words when observing and putting together this glossary. When looking up a word I was amazed to see how many meanings it had, which led me to look into these meanings, hence, the additional words in the glossary. Whilst doing this I realized how powerful words actually are. This revealed to me the important message that saying words in a certain way can bring about positive and negative energy. Therefore, what you ask for, you get, whether it is positive or negative is up to you. The final part of the glossary contains a few examples of different negative and positive thoughts and words and their affect! And a section of negative words is included to give you an understanding of how discouraging they can be.

On the final page there are some examples of affirmations!

*Look Inside
&
Find the
Gift*

Look Inside & Find the Gift

The twists and tales of life's mysteries!

The twists and tales of life, the gifts we already have within ourselves let us explore them and be amazed and surprised by what is found.

ENJOY

Let go of negativity and become aware of your gift(s)!

Sometimes something may present itself from the past, maybe even as far back as your childhood, or possibly something you have just experienced. If you do go through situations that remind you of something you have already experienced before, such as repeated situations or thought patterns. There may be some lesson to be learned from them, sometimes things you see or hear trigger off old memories of sad or unhappy moments, these will start to disappear as you remove all resistance, take control of your mind and become unattached to whatever made you feel this way in the first place, allowing negative emotions to be released.

Learning the lesson, find where it stems from, the root, the cause! Learn from it as best as you can, then it will lessen!

Clearing out old patterns and old conditions can seem difficult at first. However, once you start it becomes much easier and clearer, so use your inner guidance (intuition) to help you understand. Patterns are habits, which you can change!

Look at events that go on in your life and how they have affected you. Write down your thoughts on paper and burn them, this is a way of releasing negative emotions. Other ways of doing this are, to imagine you are sweeping out your mind or rubbing away the thoughts, making them disappear so they no longer influence you in any way, allowing for a clear state of mind. Saying releasing affirmations or talking through your circumstances with someone encourages understanding, bringing you a new perspective of easier ways of being. Also deep breathing exercises are very good too, they do help to relax the mind and body, allowing you to become more balanced within yourself.

Give yourself plenty of love and respect and allow pleasure and delight into your life right now!

Start liking/loving who you are and create within yourself the feel good factor feeling (I call this feeling the life buzz!). Discover the true you and have the quality of life you deserve. Reaffirm to yourself that negative thoughts and feelings no longer have a hold on you.

You may find you have your own way of releasing your negativity, whichever way you choose it is' BELIEVING' you can do it that is important.

Negative thoughts and words can have an effect on your body making you feel low and down about yourself. Instead of negativity fill yourself with vitality, use your willpower and discover the strength you have inside. Start acting differently towards situations by changing your perspective on them, encouraging new ways of being and understanding which will allow your confidence to shine.

So be nice to yourself, no more picking or doubting yourself as that is not good for you! Therefore have more productive thoughts that will bring about comfort not discomfort. If any negative thoughts come into your mind have a way of getting rid of them straight away!

Enjoy every moment of your life as it presents itself to you, generating a feeling of being content, comfortable and happy. Treat yourself with love and respect and see what reflects in front of you.

Always remember to love and respect others and the world around you.

Now is the time to change! Whatever the situation / experience, learning from them will guide you, inspiring better ways of being with purpose and meaningful direction, allowing better thoughts and bright ideas to flow.

Believe in the magic of your mind and the treasure in your heart!

Each time you find your mind over swamped with negative thoughts about certain aspects of your life do not fear this, instead, realise that gifts are always found in this miracle swamp of the mind. When you go into the miracle swamp it means the mind gets over swamped (filled) with negative thoughts, doubts and fears, (this is when the mind has too many thoughts in it and they get swamped and muddled!) This is what I call nattering thoughts of the mind. To get it balanced you have to slow your thoughts down so as to listen and learn. Understand and sort out/work out what is worth thinking about and what is not. Then clear away any negative thoughts and fill your mind only with positive ones. Start listening to how your mind thinks, observe and notice how your thoughts go astray. Being in control of your mind brings great satisfaction and generates a positive outlook. Turning nattering thoughts into butterfly thoughts, when released they disappear easily! This will enable you to go forward and enjoy new experiences.

Remember you are the gift, feel it inside, that magic feeling that something really exciting is happening right now.

Imagine your life as you would like it to be. Visualise amazing changes and allow them to happen. If your mind is filled with doubts and fears this will only create a negative vibe for you however, when you replace these with light, calm and loving thoughts you will generate a life full of happiness and abundance, which will allow things to manifest easily. So allow yourself to have a crystal clear mind and start creating, after all you are the one in control!

Allow yourself to become balanced and be in the presence of all your desires.

Negativity is like a fog, once lifted you can really see the beauty of life. Past memories, past patterns of thoughts, fear, doubt, worry, blame, struggle - anything negative will take you on a roundabout going nowhere. Now here in the present release all negativity from the past because all of this will hold you back. Allow all to disappear leaving you feeling new and fresh ready to explore life in a different way.

However, if you do find yourself looking back to the past in any way, always look for the goodness in what you have experienced so far and you will notice and realise many special qualities about yourself and others around you. This is what I call dancing around the edge of the miracle swamp, you have not allowed your mind to get swamped or attached, just observe always knowing you

Refund & Returns Policy

We will give a full refund on unopened goods if returned with a valid purchase receipt within 30 days of purchase.

We are happy to exchange all goods with or without a receipt for comparable products of the same or higher value (subject to any additional price being paid) i.e. they have not been opened or damaged and the goods are returned within 30 days of purchase.

Your statutory rights are not affected.

Contact Customer Services
UK: 0844 3728926
ROI: 01656 9845

Holland & Barrett Retail Ltd.
Samuel Ryder House,
7 Barling Way, Eliot Park
Nuneaton, Warwickshire, UK.
CV10 7RH.

HOLLAND & BARRETT
we're good for you

Refund & Returns Policy

We will give a full refund on unopened goods if returned with a valid purchase receipt within 30 days of purchase.

We are happy to exchange all goods with or without a receipt for comparable products of the same or higher value (subject to any additional price being paid) i.e. they have not been opened or damaged and the goods are returned within 30 days of purchase.

```
         HOLLAND & BARRETT
         SAMUEL RYDER HOUSE
        BARLING WAY, ELIOT PARK
       NUNEATON, WARWICKSHIRE
              CV10 7RH
       NEWPORT ISLE WIGHT    [3142]
             01983 525888
```

CLERK: BARBARA   18/08/11 15:53:57
RECEIPT #:3142-200252692-R2

				UNIT	EXT
LN	QTY	ITEM	VAT NOTE	PRICE	PRICE
01	1	03586	N		
		NYW WALNUT HALVES		2.19	2.19
02	1	91039	Y		
		NYW SNACK YOGURT RAI		1.59	1.59

TOTAL # OF ITEMS...   2
TOTAL AMOUNT OF SALE....   3.78

TOTAL AMOUNT 3.78

CASH   4.00
  CHANGE DUE   .22

```
   THANKS FOR SHOPPING AT HOLLAND & BARRETT
         THE NATURAL CHOICE FOR A
          HEALTHIER WAY OF LIFE
           VAT NO. 211 7273 96
```

are fine. Having no attachment when reflecting on past situations, repeated patterns, issues or occurrences, will allow you to understand yourself, see things clearer and respond with the right attitude. Everything you have experienced has brought you to who you are now. Be proud of yourself! By listening to your own intuition (inner messages) for guidance, exciting messages start to appear on the outside to guide you as well.

Encourage yourself to be balanced and allow the flow of life to be easy!

Realise the ups and downs and highs and lows of life, are lessons, experiences, all of which are things to learn from. We will refer to these as signs, that is, signs to our destiny (future). You gain knowledge and understanding from these.

Say things lightly and have no fear or doubt, replace them with loving powerful strong thoughts that will bring you in abundance the quality of life you deserve. When I say light thoughts that means no pressure or force, only gentle, easy and relaxed thoughts. Be unattached and have total trust and patience the opportunities in life are mysteries that unfold and flow to you easily.

There is a reason for everything happening at the right time. We are now in a balancing time, so allow yourself to become balanced in order for everything to be balanced in front of you. Spend some quality time, without thought and relax. Be in the now, the present, the moment here and now. This will allow the natural flow of energy to fill you with inspiration.

Once you really start enjoying every moment for what it is, everything will improve in all sorts of ways, uncovering golden treasures from within yourself. I like to call such treasure golden gems, which are good thoughts with trustworthy feelings that bring an understanding of easier ways to be, thus, uncovering amazing potential.

When you look at situations that present themselves in front of you, notice if any remind you of your past thoughts or words. You will realise by doing this, that all your thoughts and words bring to you what you asked for. However, if you stopped worrying and struggling about something, that is anything! It will automatically come to you if it is positive and disappear if it is negative.

So bring into existence the new you! Remember, the positive will always overpower the negative. Now take away the pressures and lighten up your thoughts and anything and everything will come to you. Everything happens at the right time, remember to give space and allow it to manifest.

By releasing all negativity from the mind, your life will flow along naturally in a light and easy way. You start receiving flashes of inspiration that guide you filling you with creative influence, so trust your instincts. Trust in your own ability, you are worthy!

Trust, have faith and be sure to believe in who you are!

It is your mind that creates barriers, closing the doors to anything good. Words have meaning! Listen to what you are saying, correcting any negative thoughts or words to positive and keeping them that way, (with trustworthy feelings as well!) Words are like commands so always use powerful ones. Be creative, make positive statements (affirmations) to affirm what it is you desire to say, use them in the right context giving them meaning and purpose.

Use statements that begin like these below, (add to

them whatever words that YOU desire), "I am now releasing..." "I am now attracting..." "I now have..." "I do believe..." "I am in the presence of..." "I am now experiencing..." "I am allowing..." "I can achieve..." "I am sharing ..." or "I would like ..." whichever affirmation you choose it will allow you to experience in life what you create with your mind. Affirmations are especially good to say last thing at night or first thing in the morning, use these statements for your dreams and desires. Write a few down and put them somewhere where you can see them. Affirmations can be spoken, sung or just said in your mind. They are said in a way that brings them into the present moment, right here and now. Allowing what you are asking for to materialise and be in your presence now. Believe and trust they will materialise when the time is right!

(See affirmation examples on last page of book)

The past is passed and you have presents in the presence to enjoy!

Look for positive ways to improve your life. Listen to the words you think and say start creating your life in a desirable way. Do not doubt anything, as anything is possible. Remember, everybody has special talents but sometimes they are hidden deep behind doubts and fears, which come from past conditionings, or failures that can create obstacles and feelings of being unsure. Bring into your heart and mind trustworthy feelings with good sensible thoughts. Replace fear and doubt with love and goodness, allow yourself to realise that you can achieve whatever you desire.

Turn the obstacles into options!

Talents cover a wide range of things so follow whatever you enjoy and are guided to. Discover your own natural talents, ask yourself, "What are my talents?" and allow the guidance to come to you easily keeping your mind clear for them to come in. Look for them. Create them. BRING INTO REALITY THE TRUE YOU and enjoy!

You are the seed, you are the seed planter and you are the harvester!

Use your thoughts only for positive thoughts on what you are doing right NOW, or for planting seed thoughts for your future. Seed thoughts are creating things that you would like/love to happen such as, plans, ideas, possibilities and intentions ways to improve the quality of your life in the way you choose. Do not sit around waiting for your desires and dreams to come true, continue in your everyday life and allow them to manifest naturally.

Be guided by the love you have inside, your worthiness you were born with.

Your heart's energy empowers the creation of your thoughts. Together your heart and mind use your thoughts and words to create your life experiences. Therefore, it is important, at all times, to allow positive feelings to follow positive thoughts. The feeling is TRULY BELIEVING in the magic of your mind! All thoughts and words are magic when used right because they connect and work together with your heart. Now allow everything to flow to you easily.

Seeing good reflections is being one your-self, shine goodness that comes from within.

Now Smile! Look at yourself in a full-length mirror! Looking deeply into your eyes tell yourself what an amazing person you really are and reaffirm all the special qualities you have! REMEMBER, you have released all past negativity about yourself, you are now seeing yourself anew. Always trust and believe in yourself. Discover the real you, the true you and allow yourself to shine. This strengthens your will power and opens your heart allowing shifts and changes to happen on the inside AND on the outside!

Write down:
* 5 / 10 or more, things that you are proud of yourself about
* 5 / 10 or more, things you are grateful for
* 5 / 10 things or more that you wish or desire to have
* An achievement list! ---What you would like to achieve in the near future
* Have a 'TO DO LIST' for things to do right now!

Have faith and trust in who you are!

Somebody asked me once, which made me laugh and smile, if I ever had negative thoughts about anything. My answer to this question was, "yes of course" the person appeared surprised and replied, "well you always seem so positive". This is true now. However, in the past I have experienced many ups and downs, highs and lows leading me to spend a great deal of time in the miracle swamp! Then I became aware of the gifts! One of which was the realisation that to dance around the edge of the miracle swamp was fine because it was my mind's way of revealing signs leading me to greater experiences. So whether you go into the miracle swamp or dance around the edge of it, ALWAYS know you are learning and receiving gifts of all kinds. The miracle swamp of the mind then becomes a mind of magic, bringing amazing experiences to you in a new and fresh way.

Trust your own instincts, as this is your true-self guiding you! Be light and easy with what you are thinking this will produce a calm relaxed frame of mind. Take responsibility of yourself and start progressing forward! Encourage yourself with kindness and love and become aware of your ability to do well at whatever you choose to do!

The past is past, the future unknown (to be explored!) the present is a gift to enjoy right now.

I became aware that by changing a word can give a different outlook on what you are saying for example; change "I can't do this" to "this is interesting" Making a situation 'interesting' will bring a more adventurous light to any negative experience that we have created for ourselves, by doing this we attract more of what we truly desire. My friends and I use this word in our discussions in place of any negative ones, saying "I have had an interesting day therefore, it does not matter, it is past now" (unless of course we would like to talk about it to work it out!). Remember if you are choosing to do something, say I CAN DO IT!

I have many special friends who have experienced similar situations to that of my own. Over a period of time we all realised that, when we released past-outmoded thoughts and started having a new perspective on our lives and everything around us, our own lives began to improve in many different areas. Our health has improved, we feel more vibrant and abundant in a lot of excellent ways. This is because our own hearts and minds are now working together. Our willpower has become stronger and more powerful and we have discovered the essence and energy inside of us. This will happen for you too! The more positive statements that you make the more your life will improve in such a splendid way.

Create a positive outlook for yourself and remember the past is the past, now is the time to create anew. With your heart and mind working together you can create a strong and powerful belief system that will make sure your positive thoughts remain more powerful than any negative ones. This will ensure that every time you look in front of you there is something new for you to experience and enjoy.

Nourish yourself with love and goodness!

Over the past few years I have written many messages, I shared these with my family and friends who felt they were amazing and an inspiration to them. Now they are messages in a book called 'The Golden Check Book'.

One summer evening in June 2004 my friend Ali and I decided to go for a drive around our favourite parts of the Isle of Wight, the scenery was beautiful, we had a wonderful experience watching the sunset and enjoying everything we saw, the evening was amazing. I returned home feeling wide-awake full of inspiration, I went to bed but it was impossible to sleep because my mind was filled with inspiring thoughts and messages. Luckily, I had learnt by now to keep a pen and paper close by in order to write my messages down as they were fresh in my mind, these messages were full of information and knowledge which I knew would be very useful and I felt a strong urge to write.

This exciting experience made me realise there and then, that I would write this book for everyone to read and discover who they truly are.

So it all started that night and I was very interested in what was happening, I continued to write late at night ant then put it together the next day, the more I pieced and connected together, the easier and clearer it all became.

At that time I did not have a computer or any knowledge of them at all, so Ali suggested to put it onto hers, she had a lot of faith and strong belief about what I was writing about, some nights we were up until 1or 2 o'clock in the morning I would be reading it out and Ali would do the typing. It was a great experience for both of us.

At this time Ali had a strong desire to be an English teacher and studying towards an English degree, this started to take up a lot of her time, so I knew I had to overcome my fears and learn how to use a computer myself. This was scary for me as I felt unsure of computers, so I did a short course which was helpful and had a lot of guidance from family and friends. Eventually it seemed to get a lot easier and really enjoyable.

As I worked through writing this book I had so many realisations and changes for the better, also I gained much more confidence as well. I decided that I would prefer a laptop for myself so I could do my writing anywhere. So I made a list of the things I required i.e. laptop, printer, desk etc, then I had no attachment as I knew if I was meant to have them they would arrive, appear and sure enough one by one they did (all given to me freely!) My friend bought me a beautiful old styled desk that was previously used by an Accountant/Writer! Also around the same time I was given a television and DVD player, I started to realise that when I desired, wished or required something, it would come to me if it was right for me! Now I always have a list of things which I would like to have, they either come to me freely or the financial abundance comes to me to get them. Having no attachment allows them to materialise when the time is right.

Also around this time I met some new friends – one of whom is a computer expert who has been very supportive and helped a great deal giving me computer lessons and doing the layout and cover of this book. My life has improved in so many excellent ways!

(Ali is now a qualified English teacher, and working at a school on the Island)

Start allowing and accepting good things to happen to you!

The close friends I have now, some of them have been in my life for many years. We have been getting together enjoying magical evenings of which we have called our Angel nights. Throughout our evenings we discuss different aspects of life and have decided to view life as a game. In doing this we realised that all our experiences were in fact signs, clues or messages from our inner guidance and this is why I refer to the swamp of the mind as a miracle, hence, 'the miracle mind'.

It is clear that you can create a positive future for yourself by looking easily (without struggle), for your signs and listening to your intuition that sends messages from your heart to your mind. Always have faith and trust in yourself and TRULY BELIEVE you are worthy!

Do not give up on things, Give in!

One evening my daughter Emma and I played the game 'eye spy'. After playing for a while we realised that the person looking for the object was unintentionally struggling in their mind, to find it. As soon as they stopped struggling with their thoughts, by saying "I give in", their eyes instantaneously looked towards the object. This surly shows us that when we let go, easiness flows. We were amazed by the realisation that if we allow the mind to struggle then what we are attempting to do moves further away. Once you relax the mind things become clearer. We continued to play the game of 'eye spy' my son, Marcus, joined us and the same pattern occurred over and over again with us all. This game is great to play, it makes you laugh a lot and that is good for you, have a go yourself and see!

Be the present in the presence!

I would also like to share with you a treasured experience I had with my granddaughters and how they taught me something important. When Courtney was four years old and Shannon was two they played a game together, one would say "Me" and then the other would say "Me" also. They continued to repeat this many times getting rather loud and excited about what they were saying which shows the positive effect this one word had on them. This simple game showed me the importance of the word 'Me'. I have since looked at this experience as a sign telling me that 'Yes' the 'ME' inside all of us is very special and unique. So always listen to your intuition and allow signs from the outside to inspire you and show you who you really are. My granddaughters continue to inspire me in so many special and interesting ways.

Shine goodness that comes from within you

Children show their true selves all of the time, this happens naturally. When you watch a child their eyes sparkle with a shining essence of love, goodness, and happiness. They allow life to flow along easily, enjoying all experiences. Their reactions to situations, whether positive or negative are instantaneous, the innocence of a child assures these reactions leave little or no effect. So, all feelings and emotions are released immediately. Allowing them to continue shining and flow along in their natural way! As they grow up some experiences, situations, stages of life, may leave or cause an effect that can cover up and hide their true self.

Improve your sense of well being.

Life is filled with many experiences, which can be categorised as good, bad or happy, sad. But really, all experiences are lessons about yourself and what is around you. It is up to you to enjoy and learn from them in the best way possible. Either learn from your situation or release it.

Sometimes learning to release and move forward can be a gradual experience. So be in control of your mind, allow for shifts and changes to happen and new and fresh ways to appear.

Have that sparkle in your eyes feel energized, vibrant and happy. You are what matters have faith and trust in who you are.

Believe in what you would like to achieve!

Have visualisations, use your imagination, the power of your mind, with MEANING, FEELING & BELIEVING and re-map your life in the way you choose.

You are an individual, full of many special qualities to uncover and discover. So you can shine with delight and pleasure, gaining knowledge and experience of life in an easy, flowing balanced way. Once you begin to understand yourself your life simplifies and changes with great improvement. You start gathering inspirational knowledge on your pathway and you will have realisations that change your perspective on how you feel about yourself. Things around you start to change for the better and that is because you have changed on the inside

Sow your seeds and reap the joy.

Putting things down, releasing them and giving in, brings on a light- hearted feeling which is very soothing on the mind and body, thus, creating a new and fresh self ready to experience the goodness of life. So realise that how you think and feel is what you will reflect. If you have felt clouded let the fog disappear and reveal a clear and balanced self. Now follow your instincts (intuition), these true feelings of goodness bring flashes of inspiration to guide you, by providing insights and allowing good opportunities and advantages to appear for you.

Signs, messages and clues are all around you, (suggestions from others, something you read, see or hear) seek, search, look effortlessly and you will be guided to them. Generate a positive outlook with the intention of improving yourself and what is around you right now! Trust and have faith and be sure to believe in yourself and the power of your ability to achieve success in whatever you do.

Mind and thought, heart and feeling go together, light and easy is the way to be

Start listening to the things your mind thinks about, you will realise so much about the connection between thought and action!

The lightest, calmest, easiest, thoughts, words, speech and sayings bring instant results. The light thoughts as in feel! And instant as in right now! Lighter thoughts are the ones when you think 'I have not seen so and so …. And then you see them! Or you think of someone or something and there they are or it is! This happens when your mind and feelings have no attachment to what you are thinking about. Remember the eye spy game and what happens when you struggle in your mind to find the object (making it impossible to see it)! Giving in, releases any attachment or struggle! Your reactions to things change allowing the patterns of your life to change! Have a balanced mind with good feelings, which will allow your life to flow along easily and produce effects that you desire and choose to happen!

Energy follows thought - thought turns into action - action is matter and matter is materialization!

Calmness and quickness go together with thought and action! The quick thoughts that pop into your mind as if they came from nowhere are suddenly now here, bringing insights and ideas that guide you to good opportunities. Some things come to you 'out of the blue' (automatically, instantly), revealing ideas, possibilities, ways to improve your life. Whereas some things have to be planned, organised, arranged and thought about to produce the outcome you desire.

Creative power of words!

Language! Words and their meaning! Words and their use!

Words were introduced for a reason obviously to communicate, bringing together connection and circulation. Use the right words to express what you mean! Think about words, what is said, what you are saying and the differences in the words that can be used! Rephrasing something you are going to say makes such a difference.

There are much lighter ways to get across what you wish to say, for example- instead of "I want" use "I would like" it has a lighter feel and it does have a better effect on yourself and those around you.

Here are some of examples. These are showing the effects that certain words can have!

* **'Want'** is too forceful.
* **'Need'** is pressured and heavy.
* **'Would like'** is more calming and light.
* **'Will'** is commanding, saying it strongly saying it powerfully.

* **'Require'** is nicer and has less pressure, being more orderly.
* **'Wish'** is so much lighter.

Here are some more examples of some everyday words. Changing a word can make such a difference.

Would	Want	
Can	Could	
Shall	Should	← Use these four words less or not at all
Require	Need	
Will	Would	

Refer to 'The Glossary', to look up these words in order to understand that words used in the right context do in fact give the sentence meaning and purposeful direction.

Also, look up the words of these short sentences. This will lead to more of an understanding of words and their meanings!

* What are you thinking?
* What are your thoughts?
* What is that you are saying?
* What are your intentions?
* I do believe and trust in what I can achieve!
* I am in the presence of wonderful experiences!

The amazing power of language!

I have been inspired by many writers one in particular is Lewis Carroll. In his novel 'Alice in wonderland' the sayings and riddles at the tea party are full of meaning with great significance and deliver messages to the reader / listener in easy understandable ways.

These are shown here,
* 'I say what I mean' that is the same as 'I mean what I say'.
* 'I see what I eat' is the same thing as 'I eat what I see'.
* 'I like what I get' is the same thing as 'I get what I like'.
* 'I Breathe when I sleep' is the same thing as 'I sleep when I breathe'![1]

As I was looking into words and meanings, I found Lewis Carroll's way of writing rather interesting!

Here is a collection of quotes / sayings. I am sure you will have heard of them before, short and sweet but very meaningful!

* 'As you sow so shall you reap'
* 'Ask and you shall receive'
* 'Seek and you will find'
* 'Mind over matter'
* 'It is all in the mind'
* 'Mind your own business'
* 'What you give out you get back'
* 'So far so good'
* 'All better'   (Like a parent may say to their child when they fall ove /or are hurt).

Everything comes from an idea! Everything is formed from an idea!

So you have an idea- -- -you plan it - - - you put or do whatever is necessary and what you believe possible to make or allow it to happen. Be creative! Have visualisations! Use your imagination and visualise it happening, feel the joy it brings to you and others around you. Know and believe it will happen when the time is right.

Carroll, Lewis, 'Alice in Wonderland'

Life is full of so many amazing possibilities allow them to appear naturally without pressure. So when you do think about something you would like, love to do or have, remember light and easy is the way to be.

Trust in yourself and trust in what you do!
Discover the true you!

Viewing life like a game makes YOU the inventor, the player, the actor designing your life. Be curious, and feel excited, it is your choice how you make it. Life is like a very interesting puzzle where some pieces go together so easily, whereas, others take a bit of working out LOOK, LISTEN AND LEARN. Teach yourself to think in a light calm way. Be guided by your intuition and insights, then learning becomes easy allowing things to flow better. Gradually you see the bigger picture come together and materialise in reality.

Turn visualisations into materialisations and be amazed.

Life is like a maze with the different pathways that lead you one way or another, allowing you to discover knowledge with new direction and understanding of amazing possibilities. Whatever route or pathway you take, signs and messages appear, full of meaning and purposeful direction, to guide you.

It is your choice how you make it, play it. YOU are in control, you choose!

The twists and tales of your life experiences become an exciting adventure that will inspire you. And turn the lessons of life into quests with great opportunities & peaceful pathways!

Allow life to be fun and exciting!

The starting point is you. You are the source from which your life flows.

This book has uncovered a range of subjects that interconnect that bring about connection and circulation of who you are what you are as a whole and what you can achieve.

Be in control of your feelings and emotions, use them wisely! Also use your mind sensibly! Appreciate as each moment arrives, within the moment are many treasures as well as inside you!

Right now
Feel good about yourself
Feel your presence
Be in the present
And in-joy your gifts!

Go ahead to following page to check out 'The 10 Golden Messages'!

The 10 Golden Messages For YOU!
(Effective guidelines)

1. Gift!

There are many gifts in life to enjoy. The most amazing is YOU Realise that you are the gift, full of powerful energy, goodness, beauty and love. Be the present in the presence right now!

2. Thinking in New Ways!

Letting go of the past, also old patterns and negative thoughts. Have a crystal clear mind and start thinking in a new and fresh ways (light and easy).

3. Discover the Essence Inside of You!

Your quality inside wishes to be discovered and to experience, learn to use your intuition for guidance.

4. Restore all Confidence!

Believe and trust in your own ability, be positive, you are worthy.

5. Self - motivation!

Listen to your inner self, use your will power and intuition, reaffirm to yourself that you do deserve.

6. Focus and Mind Mapping!

Be clear in your mind of your goals, be balanced and ready to explore.

7. Persistence and Pursuit!

Continually seek and follow, look for signs. You have the power to achieve.

8. Imagination and vision!

See powerful images. Be inspired.

9. Visualise and Create!

See and bring into existence right now!

10. Truly Believe!

Have faith and trust in yourself.

10 Golden Messages & Formulas

10 GOLDEN MESSAGES & FORMULAS

1 GIFT!

Becoming who you are starts with treating yourself with love and respect. You have to start with yourself that means really liking and loving who you are and everything about yourself and how you feel deep inside. It is what you think of yourself that really matters!

Realising you are the one in control, allows you to choose and create things that are right for you. Remember your worthiness it is what you were born with, you do have the ability to create the lifestyle that you desire, gaining knowledge and understanding of easier ways to be. Let go of the inner voice of fear, start listening to the inner voice of love, you will be amazed of the good effects and results that come. Nourish yourself with love fill yourself with vitality and shine.

2. THINKING IN NEW WAYS!

You are in control of your mind, in releasing the past, changing the patterns and not thinking negative any more. This will start a change for the better.

Having a clear balanced mind brings goodness to you, allowing things to flow naturally. So only have good thoughts with trustworthy feelings and start living the way you choose.

Old patterns and conditionings must disappear for new to come in. Be willing to change and allow it to happen. Observe and notice how your mind thinks, changing negative thoughts to positive ones and keeping it that way, have a new perspective towards your life. You will start to see things clearer uncovering amazing potential.

Mind and thought, heart and feeling, go together, light and easy is the way to be, you start to receive flashes of inspiration showing and guiding you to new and fresh experiences.

Have a balanced mind and fully give yourself to whatever you are doing keeping yourself in the moment, right now, here and now.

3. DISCOVER THE ESSENCE INSIDE YOU!

The essence inside you is the true you, it is your inner self, your quality, your nature and kind characteristics. It is the inner you who loves life and all its mysteries which are unfolding and revealing new experiences for you to enjoy in a remarkable way.

Understand that your inner-self, (your instinct, intuition,) does guide you with good advice, fills you with inspiration, purpose and meaningful direction. Once you start listening to your intuition such good results start to show within yourself and around you.

4. RESTORE ALL CONFIDENCE!

Your new found confidence comes from hidden within you, now you like and love who you are, your confidence starts to improve. You feel more content, comfortable and happy, ready to experience life in a delightful, pleasurable way.

Always trust and have faith and be sure to believe in yourself and the power of your ability to achieve success in whatever you do.

5. SELF - MOTIVATION!

Provide yourself with a feeling of being safe and secure. Start taking action by reaffirming to yourself that you are worthy and do deserve. Continue to strengthen your willpower and be in control of your own nature.

Your intuition brings insights, (deep understanding) influencing you in new directions, with great opportunities and advantages on your path-way.

6. FOCUS AND MIND MAPPING!

Pay attention to what your mind is thinking, making sure you have a clear frame of mind, balanced and ready to go forward in the way you choose. Generate a positive out-look with the intention of improving yourself and what is around you.

Some things come to you 'out of the blue' (instantly, automatically) revealing insights, ideas possibilities! However, some things in life have to be planned, organised, thought about, so map out and arrange in detail, express your desires by voice or writing, drawing and designing.

Your goals are your aim, purpose, intention, potential, talent, ambition, your future. Goals are reachable have determination to succeed.

Achieving them is BELIEVING in them!

7. PERSISTENCE AND PURSUIT!

Take responsibility of yourself and start progressing forward, encourage yourself with kindness and love. Find a suitable pathway that arouses interest, pleasure and delight. Think positively about everything in your life. Be ready to accept new ideas, make plans and project them forward. Putting thoughts into action and doing anything necessary to bring a good result, for yourself and others around you. Signs are always there you just have to be open (clear, light, easy way of being) to receive them, seek, search, look, ask make a request for guidance. Signs & messages come in many different forms conveying information or direction, meaning and purpose.

8. IMAGINATION AND VISION!

Expand your range or field of vision, your view, your potential, your resources, empower your visions with moral power. Become aware of your true and quick insights that guide you. Have the right attitude. Use your imagination draw pictures in your mind (visualise) forming clear visions or images of … … What you choose!

Have a vision…. Have many visions… plant the seed thoughts for your future by asking for them. Put feeling into your thoughts, ideas, beliefs, plans intentions and have a quality of life you deserve.

9. VISUALISE AND CREATE!

Use your ability now, be curious, be willing, be in control, focus your attention and say yes to the present.

Draw in your mind (project) and draw to you (attract), form and perform to appear in reality. See your future how you would like it to be. Create a desirable future opening up wonderful opportunities.

"This can happen" "it will happen", "it is happening"! Practice, have fun and enjoy.

10. TRULY BELIEVE!

Be successful in whatever you do and flourish. Appreciate yourself and who you are, use your natural ability, and do everything in light, calm easy flowing way.

So right now feel rich on the inside and be surrounded with richness on the outside which will appear in many different forms & varieties.

Be honest and truthful to yourself then goodness can come.

The Glossary.

A – Z. of amazing words.

This glossary showed me what special meanings words have, actually it amazed me to the point of looking up so many words, I was so inspired by their meanings that the glossary now plays an important role in this book.

When you look through the glossary and really start to listen to the meanings, you will realise too that when you are actually using any of these words or just thinking them the whole meaning will bring about a magic feel, they will feel more creating to say and use.

As you glance and look through the glossary, see which words you are drawn too!

Enjoy and have fun with words, put together some messages for yourself (affirmations/statements) create and choose what YOU desire!

ENJOY!

Glossary

A to Z
of
amazing words

Glossary
A to Z of amazing words

Ability: Power or capacity (to do), cleverness, talent.
Abundance: Plenty, more than enough,
Abundant, plentiful.
Accept: Receive (something offered) answer affirmatively; agree to; believe. **Acceptable:** welcome. Acceptance: accepting or being accepted.
Accomplish: Perform, carry out, succeed (in doing).
Achieve: Accomplish; reach successfully, achievement.
Acquire: Gain, get, come to have.
Advantage: Better position; superiority; gain; favourable circumstances, *take advantage of,* use (circumstance) profitable.
Adventure: Daring enterprise, exciting experience.
Affect: Move, touch (in mind or feeling); produce effect on.
Affirm: State as fact; make affirmation.
Allow: Permit; admit; give, take into consideration.
Amaze: Fill with great surprise or wonder, amazing, amazement.
Am: Person, (pres, of,) be.
Ambition: Strong desire to be successful or famous, or to do something; object of such desire. Ambitious - full of or showing ambition.
Amuse: Make time pass pleasantly for; make person laugh or smile.
Appreciate: Think highly of; be grateful for; perceive rightly; rise in value.
Appreciation: Showing gratitude or enjoyment.
Arrange: Put in order; settle; form plans; arrangement.
Are: (*presents.*) of be
Arouse: Stir up, move to action; awaken.
Ask: Put a question to; make a request (for) invite, demand.
Aspect: Way thing presents itself to sight or mind.

Assurance: Positive statement, self-confidence.
Atmosphere: Mixture of gases surrounding the earth or any heavenly body; mental or moral environment, air.
Attitude: Posture of body; settled opinion or way of thinking.
Attract: Draw towards oneself, arouse interest in or pleasure in. **Attraction:** act or power of attracting; thing that attracts.

Balance: Weigh; bring or come into a steady position.
Be (1): Exist, occur; remain, continue; have specified state or quality.
Be (2): Adding idea of all over, around, to, intensifying meaning of.
Beauty: Physical, moral or artistic harmony of which inspires admiration.
Become: Come to be; begin to be; suit, look well on.
Begin: Set about; make a start with; come into being. **Beginner:** learner. **Beginning:** time or place at which thing begins; origin, source.
Being: Existence, living person
Belief: Trust, confidence; acceptance as true or existing; what one believes.
Believe: Except as true, have faith in, trust word of.
Better: (Of good) of more excellent kind; recovering, having recovered (health), in a better way, better thing or person; improve.
Bring: Cause to come; come with or convey in any way; cause, result in, bring about, cause to happen, bring forth, give birth to, succeed in.
Bright: Shining; brilliant; cheerful; quick witted.

Calm: Still, tranquil, make or become calm. **Calmness:** calm condition.
Can: Be able to; have the right to; be permitted to.
Capable: Able, competent capable of, having fitness for, capability.
Cause: What produces an effect; ground or reason for

action; subject of interest, be cause of; make happen.
Certain: Settled; sure to happen; unfailing; sure - some.
Certainly: surely; with certainty; admittedly.
Character: (Of person, community, etc) mental or moral nature; moral strength; reputation; distinctive mark; letter; sign; person.
Chance: Way things happen, possibility; opportunity.
Cheer: Shout of encouragement or applause; frame of mind; urge on; applaud; comfort, gladden, contented, cheerful.
Clear: Transparent not clouded; distinct, intelligible; well defined; unobstructed, open; unhampered, clearly; completely, make or become clear. Clearly: distinctly; undoubtedly.
Clue: Fact, Idea, which suggest possible answer to mystery etc
Comfortable: At ease, free from hardship pain or trouble; promoting content.
Command: Order; give order; be in command; hold in check; have control of; order given. Commanding
Concentrate: Bring together to one point; focus (attention), keep mind or attention fixed (on), product of concentration.
Conduct: Behaviour; manner of conducting oneself, business, etc, *conduct,* lead, guide; control, manage; behave (oneself).
Confidence: Firm trust, sure expectations; believe in ones own ability.
Confident: Assured; bold; positive.
Conscious: Having physical and mental faculties awake and active; aware, knowing.
Conscience: Moral sense of right or wrong; awareness of moral quality of one's action and motive.
Consequence: That which follows as result or effect of something; importance; influential position.
Consider: Contemplate; think carefully about; reckon with, allow for; be of the opinion; show thoughtfulness for.

Content (1): Satisfied; pleased, willing, satisfy, contented state, satisfaction (contented), satisfied happy. Contentedness, contentment
Content (2): Capacity; amount contained; what is contained
Context: What precedes or follows word or passage and helps fix meaning.
Control: Power of command; restraint; check, supervision; device or mechanism for controlling, have control of.
Continue: Go on with; take up again; remain in existence.
Connect: Join, fasten or connect together, *connective*-serving as connection.
Create: Bring into existence; invest; originate creative.
Creation: Creating (esp. of the world); all created things; inventions.
Curious: Eager to learn, inquisitive, strange, surprising.
Curiosity: Desire to know; inquisitiveness; strange or rare thing.

Delight: Please highly; take great pleasure in (thing given), great pleasure, delightful.
Derive: Obtain or have (from a source); having starting-point or origin (from); (passive, of words), be formed from.
Deserve: Be entitled by conduct or qualities to, good, worthy of.
Design: Plan, purpose, sketch; (art of) evolving general idea, etc; scheme; pattern, form or make design (s) for; purpose, intend.
Desire: Longing; eagerness to obtain, wish or request.
Desirable: Worth wishing for; pleasing.
Determination: Determining or being determined; settled intention; resoluteness.
Discover: Obtain sight or knowledge of for the first time, find out, discoverer.

Discern: Perceive clearly with mind or senses.
Discernible/discerning: Having quick or true insight.
Do: (Does, did, done,) perform, effect; deal with, solve; make; act or proceed; be suitable for; restore.

Ease: Freedom from pain, trouble or constraint; quiet, rest; facility, relieve from pain etc; slacken; lessen or relax gradually, easily.
Easy: Not difficult; free from pain or anxiety; comfortable; gently.
Effect: Result, consequence; impression, efficiency, bring about, accomplish.
Effective: Successful in working; impressive; actual, existing.
Ego: The I, the self, self esteem.
Empower: Authorize; enable.
Emotion: Mental sensation (e.g. love, fear, hope etc); vehement or excitement, mental state, agitation. Emotional- of emotion (s); easily moved by emotion.
Energy: Force, vigour, activity, capacity for work.
Enjoy: Find pleasure in, have as advantage or benefit, experience pleasure, be happy, enjoyable, enjoyment.
Encourage: Give hope, courage or confidence to; support.
Essence: True and inmost nature of a thing; quality.
Esteem: Think highly of; consider, favourable opinion, regard.
Excite: Set in motion; stir up; move to strong emotion. Excitation: action of exciting, excitement state of being excited.
Excellent: Outstandingly good.
Experience: Knowledge gained by personal observation; events that affect one, meet with, feel, undergo.
Express: Represents by symbols etc or language; put into words; reveal, betoken, definitely stated; done, made, etc.
Expression: (Manner or mode of) expressing words, phrase, look (on face); tone (of voice); expressive

quality. **Expressive:** serving to express; full of meaning.

Faith: Trust; believe in truth; loyalty, confidence.
Feeling: Sense of touch, physical sensation; emotion; consideration for others; convictions or opinion; sympathetic; sympathies, heart-felt
Fine: Of high quality; pure, excellent.
Flow: Move, glide along, as stream; circulate; move easily; flowing; rise of tide; plentiful supply.
Focus: Point at which rays of light etc, meet; point at which object must be situated to give clear image; concentrate (mind etc).
Fortunate: Lucky and prosperous, auspicious, fortunately.
Fresh: New; not stale or faded; invigorating; just arrived; refreshing

Game: Pastime; spell of play; sporting contest; jest; spirited, ready.
Generate: Bring into existence.
Generous: Free in giving; not mean; noble mined; abundant, generosity.
Get: Obtain, earn, gain, win, procure; fetch; learn; experience, succeed in coming or going to, away etc; succeed in bringing, placing, etc, become, get on, make progress; be on friendly terms with.
Give: Handover gratuitously, make a present of; grant, deliver, pledge, devote, present, offer, be source of.
Gift: Thing given or received without payment, present; talent.
Golden: Of gold, coloured or shining like gold; precious, excellent, important.
Good: (Better, best), having right qualities, adequate, virtuous, morally excellent; worthy; proper; well behaved, agreeable, suitable; considerable, profit, well being, goodness.
Goodness: Virtue; excellence; kindness.
Great: Importance, remarkable ability.

Happen: Come about; occur by chance, happening.
Happy: Fortunate, content, glad, apt, happiness.
Have: Hold in possession; possess, contain; take, obtain; be obliged to; enjoy.
Heart: Organ which keeps up circulation of blood in the body; centre of emotions or affections; soul, mind; courage; centre or vital part, at heart, in inmost feelings, by heart, in or from memory.
Hope: Expectation and desire; trust; person, thing on which hope is based, expect and desire; feeling hope.

Idea: Picture in the mind; vague belief, fancy; plan, intention.
Image: Imitation of object's external form, esp. figure of saint etc, idol; optical appearance reflected in mirror or refracted through lens etc; mental pictures, idea, make image of; mirror; picture.
Imagination: Power of the mind forming images of objects not present to the senses; fancy; creative power of the mind.
Imagine: Form mental pictures of; suppose, think, fancy.
Improve: Make or become better.
Indeed: In truth, really.
Inner Guide: Interior, internal, act as guide to lead, direct.
Insight: Mental perception, deep understanding.
Inspiration: Creative influence, inspiring principle or person, sudden happy idea.
Inspire: Infuse (thought feeling) into; influence, animate, with (feeling idea); be source of ideas to
Instinct: Inborn tendency to behave in certain way without reasoning or training; intuition, unconscious skills, instinctive.

Intellect: Faculty of knowing and reasoning; power of thought, understanding.

Intend: Have in mind as fixed object or purpose; design, means.
Intent: Intention, *to all intents (and purposes)* practically, absorbed; eager, *intent on,* with mind and attention directed towards.
Intention: Purpose, aim, object.
Interest: Feeling of concern and curiosity; thing with which one concerns oneself; importance; advantage; arouse interest in, interesting.
Intuition: Immediate understanding by the mind without reasoning, immediate insight.
Intuitive: Of, possessing, perceived by, intuition.
Invent: Device, originate; produce or construct by original thought etc.
Is: (*Presents.*) of be

Joy: Gladden, delight, rejoice, joyful.
Jovial: Full of fun and good humour, merry, joviality.

Know: Be aware (of); be acquainted with; have information (about); recognise. Know-how, practical knowledge of methods; expertness, knowing**:** wide awake. Knowingly**:** in knowing manner; consciously, intentionally.
Knowledge: knowing; what one knows; all that is or may be known, knowledgeable, well informed.

Language: Words and their use; speech; form of speech by people; style; vocabulary; wording.
Leisure: Spare time; freedom from pressing business. Leisurely: having plenty of leisure. Leisurely: deliberate, not hurried, without hurry
Like: Like thing or person, what one likes, find agreeable or satisfactory; feel attracted by: (with should, would,) wish. Likely: Probable; to be expected to do; promising, apparently suited, probably.
Light: Natural agent that makes things visible; presence or effect of this; source of light; brightness of eyes or

aspect; mental illumination; way thing presents itself to mind, come, bring, to light, be revealed, reveal, having plenty of light, show way with light.
Light: Of little weight, not heavy; deficient in weight; easy to lift or digest or do; not clumsy; elegant; trivial, slight, fickle. **Lightly:** come by chance (upon). **Light-hearted:** cheerful.
Love: Fondness, warm affection, passion, desire; loved person or object; having love and desire (for), feel affection (for), be fond (of), delight in; admire.
Lucky: Favourable by fortune, enjoying good luck.

Make: Create, manufacture; cause to exist, bring about; cause to be, render; amount to, constitute; earn; perform, *make for*, go in direction of, *make good*, fulfil (promise etc) *make out*, write out (list etc) represents as, understand.
Manifest: Clear to sight or mind; indubitable, show plainly, manifestation.
Map: Flat representation of (part of) earth or of (part of) heaven. *Mapped,* make map of, *map out,* plan, arrange in detail.
Materialise: To appear in bodily form; become fact.
Maze: Complex and baffling network of paths, lines etc; tangle, confusion.
Mean: (Meant) Intend; be resolved; intend to convey or indicate; signify.
Means: Method, process, by which result is obtained; resources; money.
Meaning: what is meant; sense, significance, expressive, significant, meaningful
Matter: Anything that occupies space and has mass; material substance; thing(s), material; affairs, concern; importance
May: Expressing possibility, permission, request, wish etc.
Memory: Faculty by which things are recalled to or kept in mind; what is remembered.

Message: Communication sent; inspired communication.
Might: (Of May), Great power or strength or resources.
Mind: Seat of consciousness, thought, will and feeling; intellectual powers, memory; opinion; bear in mind; heed; have charge of; object (to).
Mood: State of mind or feeling
Motive: What causes person to take action, productive of motion or action.
Motivate: Supply motive or inducement to motivation.
Mysterious: Full of, wrapped in, delighting in mystery.

Naturally: In a natural way, by nature; of course.
Nature: Things essential qualities; person's innate character; kind, sort, class; (physical power causing) phenomena of material world, state of nature.
Necessary: Indispensable; that must be done; thing without life cannot be maintained; desirable thing not regarded as luxury.
New: Now first, introduced or discovered, fresh, additional; different, changed; recent, not worn.
Now: At the present time; in the immediate past, this time; the present
Nourish: Sustain with food; cherish (hope, feeling) nourishment.
Notice: Notification; heed, attention; perceive, observe.

Observe: Keep follow, adhere to; perceive, watch, take notice of; say, esp. as comment
Occur: Be met with or found in some place or condition; come about, present itself, happen; come into one's mind. Occurrence: happening; incident.
Open: Not closed; unlocked; uncovered; unfold; manifest; clear; communicative; make or become open; make start.
Open-minded: Willingness to accept new ideas.

Opportunity: Favourable juncture, good chance, opening.
Option: Choice, choosing; thing that is or may be chosen; right to choose.
Origin: Beginning or rising from something; source; extraction; starting point.
Originate: Give origin to cause to arise and begin; spring, be derived, (from, in, with) origination, originator.
Outlook: View, prospect; what seems likely to happen.

Past: Gone by; just over; expressing past action or state.
Pass: (Passed), move onwards, proceed, cause to go, change, satisfy, happen.
Peace: Freedom from, quite calm; harmonious relationship.
Perceive: Become aware of through one of the senses, esp. sight: grasp with the mind, understand.
Perception: Act of perceiving; ability to perceive.
Perceptive: Of, concerned with, perception; having insight.
Perform: Carry out; (command etc); do, act, play, performer, performing.
Persist: Continue firmly or obstinately (in course, opinion etc,) survive.
Perspective: Art of drawing so as to give effect of solidity and relative position and size; relation between visible objects, parts of subject etc; view prospects in perspective in proportion.
Person: Individual human being; man women and child; one's body or bodily presence.
Piece: Distinct part of complete whole; quantity, portion; put together, mend.
Pleasure: Feelings of satisfaction; enjoyment; sensuous gratification; will, desire, pleasurable
Plan: Drawing showing relative position and size of parts of building etc, diagram, map; project, design, *planned*, make plan of; design; arrange beforehand, scheme.

Play: Amuse oneself; engaged in games, acting etc; move about in lively way; have free movement, take part in; (games, pursuit) in light hearted way, recreation; play or act fairly; writer of play; dramatist, performing in play etc, humorous, frolicsome.
Possible: That can exist, be done, or happen; that may be or become; tolerable, reasonable, intelligible, possibly.
Possibiltiy: State or fact of being possible; thing that may exist of happen.
Positive: Definite; sure; unquestionable; absolute, confident in opinion, not negative.
Potential: That can or may come into existence or action; possible, potential resources or energy. Potentiality
Power: Ability to do or act, vigour, energy, influence; control, state with intentional influence.
Presence: Being present, being there; person's bearing or aspect, *presence of mind*, calmness, or quickness of thought and action.
Present: In place in question, here; now existing, occurring, being dealt with, etc; expressing present action etc. **Present:** Gift. **Present:** Set in conspicuous position; introduce; offer, give.
Produce: Bring forward for inspection etc, yield, give birth to; cause or bring about; make or manufacture.
Product: Thing produced by natural process or manufacture.
Productive Producing, esp. abundantly.
Progress: Forward movement; advance; development; improvement, make progress.
Project: Make plans for; throw, impel; cause (light, image, etc) to appear on the surface; thing planned to be carried out; plan, scheme.
Prospect: extensive view; mental scene; expectation, prospect, explore.
Prosper: Be successful, flourish, increase in wealth; make successful.
Prosperity: Prospering; wealth.

Prospective: Concerned with, apply to, the future; expected future.

Purpose: Object, thing intended; fact, faculty, of resolving on something, on purpose, deliberately, purpose with good etc effect or result, intend. Purposeful: Having a purpose, meaningful.

Put: Transfer to particular place; set in particular position; cause to be in some state or condition, express in words.

Puzzle: Difficult question or problem; problem or toy designed to test knowledge, skill etc, perplex, be perplexed (over), *puzzle out*, understand, solve, by exercising ingenuity, etc, puzzlement, puzzling.

Quality: Degree of excellence, relative nature or kind character, (characteristic) feature; attribute; high social position.

Reality: Being real, real existence.

Realise: Understand clearly; convert (hope plan) into fact; realization.

Really: In fact, in reality, positively.

Reason: (Fact put forward or serving as) motive, cause or justification; power of the mind to think and reach conclusions from facts etc; sense, sanity; moderation, form or try to reach conclusions by connected thought; think out. Reasonable: having sound judgement; moderate; tolerable, fair.

Receive: Accept, take, get (something offered, sent, etc); admit, welcome; entertain as guest; accept or buy.

Recreation: Refreshment of mind and body, pleasurable exercise or occupation.

Reflect: Throw back (light, heat, sound); (of mirror etc) show image (of); bring credit, discredit etc on; mediate, consider.

Relax: (Cause or allow to) be come loose or slack or limp; make or grow less severe, rigid, tense, etc,

relaxation, relaxing, recreation.
Renew: Make (as good as) new; fill up, replace; begin, make, say etc anew.
Reassure: Remove fears or doubts; restore confidence, of (person).
Request: Expression of desire for something; thing asked for, in request, sort after, ask to be given, favoured with, etc; ask.
Respect: Treat or regard with respectful conduct, esteem or honour, treat with consideration.
Response: Answer; action, feeling etc, arouse by stimulus etc, responding.
Responsibility: Being responsible, charge, trust.
Restore: Give back, make restitution of; replace; repair, alter, so as to bring back as nearly as possible to original form, state etc, bring back to dignity etc or to health, into use etc.
Rich: Wealthy, having much money, fertile, abounding *in;* splendid; highly amusing; abundant.
Right: Morally good, just, proper, correct, true; in good or normal condition; not mistaken, restore to proper position; make amend for; correct, set in order, what is just; fair treatment; fair claim; what one is entitled to; right condition; completely; justly, correctly, truly.

Say: Utter or recite in speaking voice; state, speak, tell, express; repeat, (opportunity of saying) what one has to say; share in decision, saying- remark commonly made; maxim.
Satisfaction: Satisfying or being satisfied; thing which satisfies desire or gratifies feeling; payment of debt; amends for injury. **Satisfactory:** Causing satisfaction; adequate.
Satisfy: Meet expectations or wishes of; be accepted by (person etc) as adequate; pay, fulfil, comply with; still craving of; convince; be sufficient for, satisfied, satisfying.
Seem: Have air or appearance of being; appear or be

apparently perceived or discovered to be or do.
Self 1: Person's or things own individuality or essence; (concentration on) one's own nature, state, interest or pleasure.
Self 2: Expressing reflexive action, automatic or independent action, or sameness.
Self-willed: Determination to do as one wishes, intentional action, desire.
Sensation: Consciousness of perceiving or seeming to perceive some state or condition of one's body, senses or mind; event or person arousing, excited or fear feeling.
Sense: Any of the bodily faculties (of sight, hearing, smell, taste, touch,) by which sensation is roused; feeling, consciousness; ability to perceive or feel; practical wisdom; meaning; normal state of mind, sanity.
Shall: Forming compound tenses or moods expressing futurity, command, obligation, intention etc
Shine: Emit or reflect light, glow, be brilliant.
Sign: Significant gesture, mark or device with special meaning, symbol; token, indication.
Signify: Be sign or symbol of; represent, mean, denote; announce; be important, matter.
Significant Having or conveying a meaning; full of meaning; important.
Soothe: Calm; reduce force or intensity of, soothing.
Source: Place from which stream issues; origin, cause, (of); document, etc, supplying original information, evidence, etc.
Special: Exceptional.
Spontaneous: Resulting from natural impulses; not forced, suggested or caused from outside; not deliberate or laboured, spontaneity.
Statement: Stating; thing stated.
State: Position or condition; stage of process, work etc; express, esp. fully or clearly, in speech or writing; specify.

Stage: Scene of action, perform, process, development etc, division of journey.
Subconscious: (Of) those mental activities of which one is not fully aware.
Subjective: Having its source in the mind; concerned with thought and feeling, personal.
Success: Favourable, outcome, attainment of object, wealth, fame, etc; person or thing that succeeds, successful.
Suggest: Propose for acceptance; cause (idea) to be present to mind; give hint of inkling to.
Sure: Certain confidence, convinced of having no doubt; certain to do or be; certainly.

Talent: Special aptitude, gift, mental or artistic ability, talented.
That: (*Demonstrative*) the (person, thing); the person or thing referred to, pointed to, observed, understood, etc, esp. the farther, less obvious, etc, of two, *that is (to say),* in other words; (conjunction-) introducing clause, esp. expressing result or consequence.
Thing: What is or may be the object of perception, knowledge, or thought; inanimate object; what is (to be) done, deed, occurrence; what is said; possession; affairs, matter.
Think: (Thought). Consider, be of opinion; exercise mind in active way, form connected ideas; reflect; contemplate, (think out) consider carefully and make plans, etc for.
This: (*Demonstrative*) The (person or thing) near, present, or mentioned.
Thought: (Think) Process, power, act, of thinking; what one thinks, idea, notion; consideration, heed; meditation; intention.
Treasure: Wealth or riches, highly valued thing or person, gold and gems.
Treat: Act or behave towards in specified way; deal with, apply process to, great pleasure, delight; gratification.

Trust: Confidence in or reliance on quality of person or thing, truth of statement, future state or happening, etc; credit; being trusted; responsibility, charge; put trust in; treat as reliable, trusting, trustworthy.
Truth: Being true; what is true, true statement, belief; reality, fact, truthful.

Unconscious: Not conscious; not aware (of); done, etc, without conscious action
Understand: Grasp mentally; perceive meaning of; know how to deal with, esp. from information received; take for granted.
Understanding: Intelligence, intellect, insight; agreement; stipulation, having understanding; sympathetic, tolerant
Use: Employ for purpose or as instrument or material; avail oneself of; treat in specified manner, use up, use whole of, use (right or power of), purpose for which thing can be used.

View: What is seen, scene, prospects; range of vision; mental attitude, opinion; intention, purpose (in view of) having regard to, considering, (with a view to) for the purpose of, as a step towards, look at, survey mentally, regard, consider.
Vision: Act or faculty of seeing; power of discerning future conditions etc; thing, person, etc, seen in dream or trance; supernatural apparition; sight of unusual beauty.
Visualise: Forming mental vision or image of.
Vitality: Vital power; hold on life; persistent energy, animation, liveliness.
Vitalise: Put life or animation into, infuse with vitality

Way: Road, track, path, street; place of passage; course, route, direction; distance (to be) travelled; method; manner of behaving, habit, custom, by way of.
Wealth: Abundant of possessions, riches, being rich.

What: Asking for selection from indefinite number or specification of amount, kind, etc, (exclamation) how great, how remarkable, etc, what thing (relative) that thing which. What not, anything. **Whatever:** Any (thing) at all (that); no matter what. **Whatsoever:** (More emphatic) for whatever

Why: For what reason or purpose; (relative) on account of which, expressing mild or slight surprise etc.

Well-being: Happy, healthy, prosperous conditions.

Well meaning: Having or showing good intentions.

Will (1): Forming future or conditional statement or question, wish, choose, consent to; be likely, be observed from time to time, to.

Will (2): Mental faculty directed to conscious and intentional action; act of willing; intention, determination; desire, wish.

Willing: Ready to be of use or service; done, given etc, readily, cheerfully or eager, eagerly, willingly, willingness.

Willpower: (Strength of) will, esp. power to control ones own actions.

Wise: Having, showing, sound judgement resulting from experience and knowledge.

Wish: (Expression of) desire; thing desired; request; expression of desire for another's happiness, success etc, have or express wish (for).

Wonder: Strange or remarkable thing; event, etc; miracle, prodigy; emotion aroused by novel or unexpected thing; astonishment, be affected with wonder; feel doubt or curiosity, be desirous to know or learn.

Wonderful: Marvellous, surprising; surprisingly fine, excellent.

Word: Written or printed symbol(s) representing sound(s) having meaning and constituting smallest possible element of language; things said, speech etc; tiding; command; promise, assurance, word for word exact(ly), word of honour, put into words to express, select words to express.

Wording: Form of words used, phrasing.
Worthy: Deserving, respect, deserving of, of sufficient worth, merit etc, worthiness.
World: Human existence, *this* present life; earth; planet or other heavenly body; universe; everything, all people; human society; sphere of interest, action or thought; vast amount or extent.
Would: (See will) would be, desiring or professing to be.

Zest: Piquancy; keen interest or enjoyment, relish, gusto

Below is an example of what both, positive and negative thoughts and words carry with them and the effects they do have on you.

Positive:	Negative:
* Vibes: Good atmosphere,	*Vibes: Bad atmosphere,
* Clearness/Openness,	* Blocked/Barriers,
* Light feeling,	* Heavy feeling,
* Unlimited abundance,	*Un-desired baggage,
* Trust,	* Worry,
* Assurance,	* Stress,
* Easiness,	* Pressure,
* Wonderful feelings,	* Low festering feelings,
* Shining,	* Dull,
* Love,	* Fear,
* Goodness,	* Doubt,
* Happiness,	* Sadness,

Always remember positive feelings with positive thoughts and words!

What I am saying here is your mind is like a computer, whatever you tell it, it believes. So whatever thoughts or words you use will bring an effect. So realise that even a mere little thought (whatever… and there it is…… materialised!)

I have included this small section of negative words and their meanings, showing you what not to be or say and live your life in a better way!

Anger: Feeling or showing anger; (of wound, cut etc,) inflamed.
Anxiety: Feeling of dread and uncertainty about the future.
Discomfort: Uneasiness of body and mind, lack of comfort
Distress: Mental anguish; pressure of want, danger or fatigue, cause severe strain to, exhaust.
Doubt: Feeling of uncertainty: undecided frame of mind; inclination to disbelief; uncertain state; be in doubt on; mistrust.
Fear: Emotion caused by impending alarm, dread, be afraid (of) be anxious.
Hate: Dislike strongly, hatred – active dislike; ill will.
Need: Want, requirement; necessity (of); time of difficulty; destitution; poverty, be in need of, require; be under necessity to do.
Negative: Expressing or implying denial or refusal; lacking positive attributes; opposite to positive, negative statement, word quality etc.
Obstacle: Hindrance; something that stands in the way.
Stress: Pressure, tension, strain, greater force used in uttering syllable etc. Lay stress on; emphasize.
Struggle: Make ones way with difficulty; strive hard; struggling; effect under difficulties.
Try: Test, make severe demand on; attempt Trying: Esp. exhausting exasperating; difficult to bear.
Uneasy: Restless, troubled, anxious; uncomfortable in mind, uneasiness.
Unsettled: Disturb; make restless, anxious.
Want: Lack, absence, need, (of); destitution; need; something needed or desired; require; desire, wish possessions or presence of, want for, lack, be without.

Wanting: (Esp.) lacking in; lacking, without.
Worry: Cause of anxiety or concern; troubles, uneasy.

These are surely showing you the different feelings and emotions that go with the words and meanings and the effects they have on you! So it is best to avoid them.

Creative power of words!

Notice the special qualities of words!
How they are expressed!
In everyday life
Experiences!

Here are some examples of affirmations!

* I am now releasing all negative thoughts and feelings, allowing myself to feel balanced.
* I am now attracting good things to me.
* I now have trust in myself and faith in what I do.
* I do believe I am fit and healthy.
* I am in the presence of wonderful experiences.
* I am now experiencing delight and pleasure.
* I am allowing myself to feel content, comfortable and happy.
* I can achieve whatever I choose to do.
* I am sharing my abundance with others.
* I would like/love my desires and ideas to materialise right now.
* I have faith and trust in whatever I am doing, bringing abundance, prosperity, love and happiness.
* Throughout my day I will be calm, relaxed, balanced and happy, full of love, fun and inspiration.
* I now feel balanced, ready to explore life and experience enjoyment.
* I believe I can succeed in what I choose to do.

Explore the possibilities of life!

Now you have read this book, I suggest you read through it and play with it, as many times as you like.

May your desires and wishes come true!

Amen.

Sharon Duvall"s book is a great way to begin thinking in a more positive fashion. If we all spoke more carefully, perhaps life would manifest itself in a better way.
Chris Alexander

An amazingly intuitive book written by an amazing woman. Whole new pathways are opening to me and more than ever I appreciate the importance of positivity in all things.
Jackie Atkinson

Truly the most life changing book you will ever set eyes upon.
Kay Tosdevin

The message that Sharon delivers in this book is uncomplicated, yet profound – that 'you are the source from which your life flows.' She believes that the way in which you view yourself has a direct impact on the quality and purpose of your own life and that of others. By adjusting the way in which you think, act and speak - on a daily basis - you can discover the power to attract the quality of life that you deserve. Enjoy!
Jacqueline King

A lovely Light for the soul to follow.
Julia Hayles